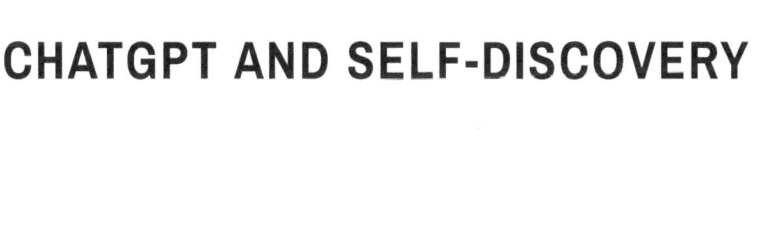

CHATGPT AND SELF-DISCOVERY

Finding Your Purpose

BILL VINCENT

RWG Publishing

CONTENTS

1. Introduction — 1
2. Understanding Self-Discovery — 3
3. Exploring ChatGPT as a Tool — 5
4. Benefits of Using ChatGPT for Self-Discovery — 7
5. Limitations and Considerations — 9
6. Setting Intentions for Self-Discovery — 11
7. Reflecting on Personal Values and Passions — 13
8. Identifying Strengths and Weaknesses — 15
9. Clarifying Life Goals and Aspirations — 17
10. Overcoming Obstacles and Challenges — 19
11. Exploring Different Paths and Possibilities — 21
12. Seeking Guidance and Support — 23
13. Taking Action and Implementing Changes — 25
14. Evaluating Progress and Adjusting Course — 27
15. Integrating Self-Discovery into Daily Life — 29
16. Conclusion — 31

Copyright © 2024 by Bill Vincent

All rights reserved. No part of this book may be reproduced in any manner whatsoever without written permission except in the case of brief quotations embodied in critical articles and reviews.

First Printing, 2024

CHAPTER 1

Introduction

Oftentimes, the answers to the big questions of your life are within yourself. Despite this, the nagging questions can get in the way of moving forward when it seems that the world, known and unknown, is waiting for you. Why am I the way that I am? What do I want to do? How do I want to spend my time? What am I meant to do? The best answers to big questions usually come from honest conversations with close friends, strangers, serendipitous events, deep personal experiences, or if you are lucky, a quiet walk in the forest. Sometimes, the answers come from within yourself, when you ask yourself the right question at the right time. But why can't an AI give you some insights or at least nod you in the right direction? With ChatGPT's capabilities of a dialog engine and creativity, there might be some novel, helpful, or mind-altering information hidden in there somewhere. Since everything in life might have mundane or miracle potential, why can't you give talking to ChatGPT a try?

Do you ever wonder what your unique purpose is in this world? I'll spoil the surprise - you are here to experience life, given the unique perspective that only you have! I know that's abstract and unfulfilling, but that's where self-discovery comes in. Finding your purpose isn't an endpoint or destination, but a process - a journey. In this thought-provoking article, I bring two powerful concepts together to help you (and others) along this journey. The first notion is self-discovery: "The actions of a person when seeking his or her true self, resulting in self-awareness, joy, peace, direction, and fulfillment." This definition comes from David Mecham's book, The Missing Self. The second concept is OpenAI's GPT-3, a word-based artificial intelligence that has the naturalness of natural language processing (NLP) that is breathtaking. While humans google questions they ask themselves, what if they dared ask these same questions to an AI? Can a natural language AI, like ChatGPT, provide obvious, unexplored, or otherwise tantalizing advice on self-discovery?

CHAPTER 2

Understanding Self-Discovery

Being aware of one's own feelings is one of the basics of emotional self-regulation. In addition, when we are aware of our own emotions, thoughts, and feelings, we can manage them effectively, which makes it easier for us to make decisions and direct attitudes according to our beliefs and values. For self-knowledge skills, we need to know how to receive feedback, valuing the opinions of others. We need to face life in a positive way, managing our emotions, and starting to reconstruct what we know about our experiences, to value the fact of looking at one's own feelings and emotions, always thinking about one-to-one communication. It is a giant step in the process of self-discovery. There is no magic formula for self-knowing skills, but when we begin to observe our behaviors and feelings, our self-knowledge will begin to be developed.

Self-discovery is a conscious effort to find your needs, wants, and desires through insight and reflection. The journey to self-discovery happens through the following stages: the time comes when you must decide who you are, the problems are solved by decision, the time comes when you decide what you have to do, the one who gives life to the answer is you, be respectful and cultivate the heart, search for other perspectives, and adaptation to new living dynamics. When you make this process of self-discovery, that is, of self-knowledge, you are able to strengthen and align your thoughts, feelings, actions, and personal desires, which favors harmony in your decision making, becoming an assertive individual. A principle to know yourself, to identify your capabilities, to develop emotional intelligence and self-esteem. It is valid to point out that self-discovery is not only when something goes wrong, it can and should happen throughout life, to promote growth and introspection.

CHAPTER 3

Exploring ChatGPT as a Tool

3.2 Interacting with ChatGPT. When you engage in self-reflective, self-discovering dialogue, or check-in with questions as part of your practice, remember to avoid leading or yes/no questions, leave space for the response of who you are dialoguing with and their rhythm, and focus on the conversation between yourself and who you are connecting with. If you are also being in self-reflective stillness, silence, or dialogue with others with different methods, keep reminding yourself about that in self-discovery, context (with your clients, in the business organization or setting, with a group, or individually, any of you, etc.) matters. What you focus on, from where and what you ask and intend, the kind of context or container you design for yourself and your creation, the different levels or range of inquiry - all options and their choices will impact and transform in unique and intertwined ways. Some of the questions we explored with ChatGPT are representative of a wider range of topics - starting from introductory self-discovering dialogue with ChatGPT, then self-discovering deeper aspects related to purpose, and, finally, evolving toward self-organizing development, coaching, and environmental context.

3. Exploring ChatGPT as a Tool. 3.1 Context. I recently explored ChatGPT as a tool for self-discovery with some peers. These peers are also coaches or aspiring coaches who already have experience using different models they've been trained in (e.g., Integral Coaching, Co-active Coaching, PNI in coaching, etc.). Our chat with ChatGPT was in English with a 3 paragraphs to one page maximum length. ChatGPT (GPT-3) took about 15 seconds to respond. We also periodically added more context about our work and perspective, to have ChatGPT answer from a more informed place about us as coaches or human beings. This exploration aimed to stretch our minds, learn to integrate ChatGPT within our own current or future coaching practices, and keep opening up the positive and negative sides of working with any tool. The starting point was to have a conversation with ChatGPT around self-discovery and coaching.

CHAPTER 4

Benefits of Using ChatGPT for Self-Discovery

Another benefit of using ChatGPT relative to people in our environment is the fact that ChatGPT does not have an agenda or is influenced by previous knowledge of your characteristics. It does not have a set of idiosyncratic ideas to motivate its place in society because it has none. It is just trying to put you in touch with what your society programming has already figured out about your inner workings. This is helpful because it maintains critical contact with your already figured out inner workings and not the set of quirks of your friend, therapist, favorite life coach, etc. This way, you are never a shadow of someone else's vision of who you should be – using ChatGPT seems like a purer form of interacting with your essence with minimal disruption. More than a few clients have reported this fact to me as they interacted with me about their experience.

After engaging with many different people at ChatGPT, it's apparent that using ChatGPT for self-discovery comes with many benefits. The first reason, and arguably one of the key factors, is the non-judgmental and non-direct way that your purpose is finally revealed. Discovering your purpose is not a task that one should take lightly – it takes honest communication and some probing to finally understand your purpose in life. ChatGPT allows you to work through this process cogently, without feeling judged, rushed, or confused by the process. We are all programmed to realize our purpose, so the outcome is never a surprise, but its revelation is timely and I'd say therapeutic.

CHAPTER 5

Limitations and Considerations

Even with these limitations, we note that we were able to demonstrate the potential of measuring self-discovery data in realtime at a large scale, paving the way for future computer-mediated self-discovery research across a variety of non-English-speaking communities accessible through different digital environments. Instead of focusing on natural language understanding and modeling, we had to collect and aggregate prompts using relatively simple TF-IDF based approaches due to methodological constraints. Since we know that certain phrases are more typical of certain types of self-discovery (e.g., "find purpose"), we believe that it should be possible for researchers to collect and generalize more purpose-specific prompts (e.g., probes or interventions) from datasets like ours and apply data-driven results directly to their studies. Finally, to enrich our understanding of self-discovery and well-being, the diversity and background conversations linked to the chats should be contextualized, which means we need to draw a comprehensive understanding of how these findings might fit into what we already know about well-being and cultural differences.

To close, we also acknowledge the study limitations. Given the nature and complexity of the dataset, computational and methodological constraints are one of the main limitations. First, although we used the latest version of ChatGPT (4), we only used the web-based online interface, which does not have fine-tuned parameters needed to address very open-ended instructions, and may not be as human-like as it could be. Second, even though we had scraped and filtered a large collection of discussion prompts from popular social media (Tumblr and Reddit), we only used a tiny subset of 153 prompts. Third, the data we analyzed was relatively homogeneous, involving English speakers participating within sex- or age-based communities and was gathered before the COVID-19 pandemic. Finally, we had limited means for how our method results could be validated. One solution for future studies could be to use other NLP methods or experiments in which people engage a human listener.

CHAPTER 6

Setting Intentions for Self-Discovery

Among those participants who experienced facilitation, for some people the generative chatbot was a deep and intense experience, as it brought forth emotions either previously thought, felt, or subconscious thinking into conscious awareness. I found that although some people may be skeptical about chatbots facilitating self-discovery, the interview and review findings suggested that a generative chatbot is capable of handling those participants who are willing to engage with the right mindset. In participants who approached the chatbot experience with curiosity and openness, the chatbot indeed facilitated reflection. Specifically, participants who explicitly set their intentions for reflective chat sessions and take them seriously seem better able to engage in self-discovery. The themes that emerged from the chatbot sessions seemed truly reflective of the interviewees' already established introspective nature, as their curiosity may have subsequently enhanced their level of particularly reflective engagement with the chatbot. Understandably, if people are not quite willing to take the chatbot seriously as a tool for reflection in self-discovery, their participation in the chatbot's sessions might just turn out to be mere chit-chat.

Now, you might understand a bit more about generative chatbots and self-discovery. The chatbot is programmed in such a way that it helps people to think and reflect on existential matters. In my interviews, many participants were already engaged in reflection on the meaning of life and self-discovery, and had plenty of existential questions. And, of course, a chatbot isn't going to be able to provide clear answers. In essence, the key to self-discovery with a chatbot lies within the motivation and preparedness of the participants. Indeed, the participants and their self-generative intentions for self-discovery are the driving force behind the chatbot's efficacy.

CHAPTER 7

Reflecting on Personal Values and Passions

I would take a moment to list out any and all values that resonate with you. This isn't just "hard work" or "integrity," although they can be if it truly is the thing that fills up your gas tank. Also sprinkle in hobbies, personality traits, and other experiences that you have had. There is no rush here! This exercise will lead you to think about the personal essay you'll write to accompany your college application, the mission statement your company will create, or how to turn your internal value system into activities that take you closer to the impact you want to make. As you're able to draw out this list of values, take a look at your roles and your personal values that make an impact towards others. This leads to a variety of activities. These values might help you best by teaching and mentoring. Startup founders could form a company centered around philanthropy or could create a solution that benefits people in a way that makes the founder's heart sing. What can you do to make sure that you're working on activities tied to your values?

You have now made it past the halfway point of this book, and I hope your mind is buzzing with ideas. At this stage, I would encourage you to spend some time thinking about any patterns you're observing. Which activities, roles, and values you've articulated are resonating with you the most? Which of them make you feel the happiest, the most energized, the most fulfilled? In contrast, which of them make you feel drained, uncomfortable, or like you're not making your greatest impact? And are there any themes in the incongruent ones? In other words, what is it that is emotionally driving you? This next visual exercise that I have for you focuses on reflecting on these personal values and passions.

CHAPTER 8

Identifying Strengths and Weaknesses

On the other hand, people often get caught in the game of comparison. However, anyone who really wants to assure an individual on their actual weakness should try to identify it, after all. And we should identify potential areas that need growth and upgrades. One can take the help of three key traits. The first trait is curiosity. If they ask tons of questions, do they want to understand why? In what ways and details about how their environment and everything works around them? This demonstrates the eagerness to dive in deeper beyond the surface level. It really defines one's inner drive to know. This helps to understand others better, become a better partner, a person, and even a better communicator.

Everyone has certain strengths. You might be personable and enjoy talking to strangers, which can lead to forming deeper relationships, successful socializing, and marketing. Other people may aspire to be in a more creative artistic role, and others may enjoy analytical math and engineering jobs. What's most important is that your strength should define who you really are. If you are unsure which roles you excel in, there are many guides available to help you discover your strengths and put them to work!

CHAPTER 9

Clarifying Life Goals and Aspirations

Until these types of goals are clarified, time and effort is often wasted on reaching goals and making decisions that are not aligned with one's dreams. For many SAD sufferers, childhood issues such as maltreatment and dismissive or fearsome attachment styles can hinder the evolution of clear and attainable life goals. If you think that early aspirations and goals were forged by controlling individuals with an arm's length from you and/or were based on fears of rejection, living a life that creates a joyful and fulfilling existence is not likely to be possible. Many individuals initially try to bypass earlier life goals and ignore resulting insecurities, deceptions, and difficult emotions in the hopes of living in the "now". However, upholstering one's life with "in the now" decorations alone does not lead to living a joyful and meaningful life, a life that can be savored in the long term. To pave the way to living an authentic life, you will first need to invest time and energy into understanding your strengths, personal values, and innermost aspirations. The reward for this effort will be the construction of a bridge connecting where you stand with your meaningful, fulfilling personal or professional destination.

To achieve your desired life goals and pursue your professional aspirations, it is important to first clarify exactly what these goals and aspirations are in the first place. Because many individuals who suffer from SAD face roadblocks when trying to clarify and/or commit to deep life goals and professional aspirations, it is important not to become prematurely discouraged if difficulties are experienced during the following steps.

CHAPTER 10

Overcoming Obstacles and Challenges

But the reality of our tasks actually isn't so difficult. Overcoming our obstacles and challenges may seem like a daunting enterprise, but that usually isn't the case. Our goals are often much more manageable than that; it's simply the blinders on our vision that make them so formidable. So it's up to each of us to make them less so: Take the reins of your life and steer them through ambitious, yet realistic aim. You know yourself better than anyone. You probably know what it is that you really enjoy. As such, what you should consider doing is casting off those silly fears of the unknown and journey forth, unashamedly towards whatever it is you desire. Know that your destination may change over time; knowing that creating new goals is the nature of living a life of passion. As such, whenever you find that your goals are no longer serving you, simply change them.

Overcoming Obstacles and Challenges. Guiding ourselves away from a life of escapism and towards a life of passion can be a real challenge. After all, escapism is an addiction and an addiction is fairly hard to overcome! Not only is there the time investment required to overcome any bad habit, there's also the pain involved in breaking free.

Feeling lost and unable to find purpose for our lives is a problem that seems to afflict a growing number of individuals. In the following 34-part series, we address this issue, presenting a variety of ways to discover your own personal reason for being.

CHAPTER 11

Exploring Different Paths and Possibilities

The second avenue is exploring what you excel at, or at least what you might pursue, with some effort and dedication, to render yourself greater benefit. Here you may want to consider your various skills, talents, and proclivities only evident when you are thoroughly enjoying the activity. Many people find a particular hobby or craft particularly relaxing, fulfilling, or worthy of their time and effort. This provides a hint to what they might want to consider pursuing. Sleep easy at night knowing your "want" with respect to yourself includes what you are good at, and quite enjoy doing. A satisfying job takes into account your abilities as well as other logistical parameters. There is no hard and fast rule about this, and I don't know of any specific research findings to support these assertions. However, considering your wants and the needs and wants of others you might seek to fulfill might be a great place to start.

The first avenue is quite direct. What do you want? While this seems simple, it sometimes takes a little asking and digging. For now, we'll use wants, wishes, and desires somewhat interchangeably.

In creating your emergent self, you have three main avenues of influence. Although using them thoughtfully and deliberately is usually necessary to reach your full potential, none produce the whole picture alone. For best results, you may find it helpful to intermingle these different aspects of yourself, understanding that the emergent you comes into being on these terms and should not be rushed. This journey is highly individual and yours alone, though along the way you may meet others traveling with you who are on their respective paths. Or perhaps, new to their discovery and willing to wander a while with you on yours.

CHAPTER 12

Seeking Guidance and Support

Whether it's surrounding yourself with supportive people who are a few steps ahead of you or reminding yourself how their story started (guess what - often times they didn't have it all figured out either), this could become a challenging but rewarding journey to reshape the way you typically ring in the new year. Before you dive into your new year objectives, start with finding your purpose as it's something that will influence every aspect of your life and guide all decisions to follow. I sincerely hope you enjoy this guide and that it brings you a little closer to seeing your unique path. Even when your goals aren't fully defined or you're working on truly understanding your purpose, here's to approaching the new and even scary - with fierce compassion and embarking on a year that's worth remembering.

If you still feel lost and find yourself asking deep-rooted questions, sometimes the best way to arrive at answers is to seek guidance from those who inspire you. Are there certain writers whose work speaks to you in ways you can't explain? Are there people you know whose career, creative outlets, and contributions are in line with what you'd like to do one day? What advice do they typically share online? See if you can connect with them and learn more about the path they've taken. I know that from time to time I reach out to a few people I have deep respect for, and their insight, or even a casual word of encouragement, has always helped me when I needed to shift my perspective back to a better approach.

CHAPTER 13

Taking Action and Implementing Changes

If you are clear you have to endow enduring traits, and you recognize that developing these traits is the most satisfying way to live your life, all that is left is to resurrect Sisyphus, beginning with the burden of self-definition and finding true fulfillment. Most people do not enhance their focus, control behavior to align or control learnings, or continually think about their strategic pursuits. Yet if we focus on building self-directed learners - educate them - the rest will come. Development will occur as students work towards their goals, and self-directed learners naturally become independent and active learners. Part of this is that the self-directed nature of chatbots (learning-centered and focusing on self-discovery, a subset of personal insights) helps to promote self-reflection and self-direction - a key ingredient for self-improvement.

Once we understand how we want to be or become, what action tends to flow without needing further clarity? What practical steps should we consider to produce these changes? These questions are important because refining your practice of change until it becomes a habit will lead you into the territory of powerful self-definition. These are the practices that reflect the meaning and purpose in your life. They become part of you, defining what matters the most to you. By taking action and implementing these changes, you are already living the definition of the purpose you seek to make complete. How are you developing the enduring traits you need to become what you aspire to be?

CHAPTER 14

Evaluating Progress and Adjusting Course

With the help of a Support Program (RAP) model, the next Survey section revisited these principles after the deep dive and benefits discussion, adapted the language to be more general, applied it to our relationships as well as ourselves, and focused on particular actions which clearly benefited our sense of purpose in a number of simple but very salient ways. Having rebuilt each connecting facet of our purposeful living architecture in practical ways we could relate to and make judgments on, and without having to use or even make empty value judgments at all, we were able to then make exoteric, empirically testable predictions about what should happen if our particular sense of purpose was, indeed, good or well-formed or whatever "right" might have meant here. Our unique blend of support program and deeper student experiences is designed to help us, "put our money where our mouth is," in terms of numerous such predictions. Here, I only ask if they seem reasonable to you.

How might you evaluate your journey of self-discovery so far? How far have you come, how well are you now showing up to the world, and what could you do to improve your journey moving forward, if you so wish? To evaluate progress, let us return to the itself. To embody a real version of your Big Self, how well are you now doing, relative to where you were before, with respect to the seven principles of purposeful living arising back from the overview?

CHAPTER 15

Integrating Self-Discovery into Daily Life

One of the creative exercises we have used in James, the other School Counselor and I have done is handed you a blank board with markers out. When handed a task to write your life purpose on a large board – perhaps on a funeral hall, I often see our students floored and sometimes even frazzled. However, the prompt to write your purpose or passion on a very personal item, can be less abrasive and sparks more intuitive responses than you might think. By providing you with a T-shirt, or a tube of chapstick, or even a lunchbag, we prompted you to share what was really most important to you. It is almost like creating a time capsule or a piece of history that you revisit and may be eventually change or add to over the years. While the medium can start a bit intimidating, with encouragement in the form of prompts to push the understanding of your passions even further, insightful answers surface as you make deeper and more intimate connections with your life. A doable idea is to start an exercise like ribbon therapy or other similar activities to help make those connections and make a connection with our purpose today.

You probably have a lot to think about after the activities of the last 4 weeks. We have learned a lot through many experiences – successes, maybe some failures – but many important experiences that we can reflect upon to really help maybe guide the direction of our purpose. Now, it is important to begin to integrate this self-discovery into the process. One way to do this is to reflect upon the following questions. First, you might want to ask yourself "What exactly is my current purpose?" and then we will reflect upon other questions as well. So, "What exactly is my current purpose or life passion?" Take a moment to think about that. "And how do I know, how have I come to this understanding?" If the answer comes easily to you, it is generally because you have taken your values into deep consideration or instinctively highlighted instinctive strength; however, there could be a thousand reasons why you are able to answer this question easily. Proceed to ask yourself "What are the differences between your past and current purpose statements?" From there, ask yourself "What is missing in your life today?" Finally, "What's stopping you from reaching your purpose today and how can you overcome these barriers? These are a lot of questions to think about and ask yourself but they are really important to reflect upon and consider. So, now let's talk about some exercises and activities that could help deepen our understanding of our purpose.

CHAPTER 16

Conclusion

There are many important clarifications and caveats here since, even if personal identity and purpose is very high-leverage, that doesn't directly translate to high leverage in promoting realization and purpose in some particular very-hard-to-change world system way. One reasonable step to promote self-realization and purpose in the future direction of the economy is to research and develop advanced AI. This could accelerate the purpose-finding process for those who use AI. (Though also conversely retard it if they overlearned to be mentally dependent on AI.) Furthermore, AI could decrease the task pressure for people, making it minutely easier to find purpose. This also relates to other research agendas: Some support the long, rather than short, path to purpose, either due to the hope that compounding wisdom means that those with years of experience are most likely to be wise (and so it is good if we spend a great many years of horrid drudgery slaving away before we are useful contributors to society), or due to the hope that wisdom can come from unspecified hard problems which result if there was a lack of useful personal problems.

The key insight of this chapter, and in fact the research of our ESCoE ChatGPT team (and much of the AI-impacts community), is that the internal, psychological change - self-realization and purpose - is the most substantial transformation of economic structure. Once everyone has this change, no more substantial changes are left. This is why it's major and happens to everyone in their lifetimes, but in terms of actual capabilities, it's small. It doesn't change anything in the objective world except for small lifestyle adjustments. It doesn't affect economic or production volume structure or anything else we've mentioned as a substantial transformation. It is the final transformation; we've run out of others before we run out of time.

Milton Keynes UK
Ingram Content Group UK Ltd.
UKHW030908271124
451618UK00011B/327